The Collectors

MARIJULIA LLOYD

Edited by
Peter Beynon

Published in association with the Adult Literacy and Basic
Skills Unit

Hodder & Stoughton

LONDON SYDNEY AUCKLAND TORONTO

ISBN 0 340 52207 0

First published 1990

Typeset by Wearside Tradespools, Fulwell, Sunderland
Printed for the educational publishing division of Hodder and Stoughton Ltd, Mill Road, Dunton Green, Sevenoaks, Kent by St Edmundsbury Press Ltd, Bury St Edmunds, Suffolk

*P*rofessor Scott had taught Biology for twenty years.
He knew that his students at the University
learned more quickly
if they collected their own specimens.

Once a year he took a group to Carmen Beach,
to collect plants and animals.
The beach was on a remote part of the Gulf of Mexico.
It took a day to drive there from Vera Cruz.

The group was going to spend four days at the beach,
but Maria was worried.
She had heard strange things about the area.

Anna noticed that something was wrong.
'What's the problem, Maria? Don't you like the sea-side?'

'Of course I do,' said Maria,
'but haven't you heard about the Nichols case?'
'No,' said Anna.

Maria gave her a hard look.
'Well, you'd better listen. It's really scary.
Four months ago a man called Andrew Nichols
went on a fishing trip to the Gulf.
He went with his partner, Clay Connors.
They set up camp at Carmen Beach.
The next week
Connors was found wandering along the beach,
ten miles away.
He had lost his memory
and Nichols had vanished.
The police searched all along the coast,
but didn't find anything.'

'So a man disappeared.
It's nothing to do with us,' said Anna.
'Look,' said Maria,
'I just have a bad feeling about this trip.'
'You can be such a baby,' said Anna,
walking out of the room.

*   *   *

4

A week later, the students arrived at Carmen Beach.
They found a good place near the beach to make camp.
They put up the six tents in a semicircle.

It was now five o'clock. Maria was exhausted.
She crawled into her tent
and started to unroll her sleeping bag.

'A little nap is just what I need,' she thought.

'Right,' said Professor Scott.
'We've just got time for a walk along the beach
before it gets dark.
I want to show you a colony of clams.'

Maria sighed and crawled out of the tent.

Pablo Ramon, the Professor's assistant,
was standing outside.

'Come on, lazybones,' he said, helping Maria to her feet.

Maria fancied Pablo
but she was too shy to do anything about it.
Her face went bright red.
Pablo smiled.

The Professor was already walking towards the beach
with the other students.
Pablo and Maria followed.

6

As they reached the beach,
Pablo saw something in the sky.

'Look, Professor,' he shouted.

Far out over the sea,
something strange hung in the sky.
It was cigar-shaped and silver in colour,
with flashing red lights along the side.

'That? It's a weather balloon,' said the Professor.

The thing then started to make a buzzing noise,
like a swarm of bees.
Slowly it sank down in the sky
and disappeared under the water.

'That was no weather balloon,' said Maria.
'That was a U.F.O.'

But the Professor had already moved on,
looking for the clams.
He hadn't seen what had happened.

The students looked at each other.
'I must be dreaming,' said Pablo.
'I'm a scientist.
I don't believe in U.F.O.s
or little green men from outer space.'

8

Maria was too shocked to say anything.
But her mind was going at a hundred miles an hour.
The Nichols case!

The students followed the Professor.
They found the colony of clams
and the Professor gave them a lecture.
But they weren't listening.
They were thinking about the silver object
and the way it had disappeared into the sea.

The lecture finished
and the Professor led them back to the camp
like a flock of lost sheep.

As they reached the tents,
a thick fog came rolling in from the sea.

'What the hell's happening?' said Pablo.

'Ah, the weather around here is rather unusual,'
said the Professor.

And then *they* arrived.

Walking out of the fog, walking from the sea.
Three tall figures, wearing silver uniforms and gold boots.
On their wrists they had bracelets with flashing buttons.

Their faces were golden brown.
They had long red hair
and their eyes sparkled like diamonds.
There were two men and a woman.

'They look like actors from *Star Trek*,'
Pablo whispered to Maria.

Maria shook her head.
'No, these are aliens.'

'What do you want?' said the Professor.

The visitors looked at each other.
The woman stepped forward
and pushed a button on her bracelet.

'My name is Kal, and these are Thor and Zov,' she said,
waving a hand at the two men.
'We have come from the planet Utopia
in the Andromeda Galaxy.'

12

The Professor turned to the students and laughed.
'That's a good joke,' he said.

'This is no joke, Professor Scott,' said Kal.

'How do you know my name?' he said.
He sounded frightened.

'We know many things, Professor.
We know that you are here with your students
on a field trip.
You have come here to collect specimens.'

Maria felt sick. Was this really happening?
No. It was a dream.
She pinched herself.
'Ow!'

Kal turned to look at Maria.

'No, Maria. This isn't a dream.
This is real.'

Maria wanted to run,
but her legs wouldn't move.

'What do you want?' said the Professor again.

'We are alike, you and I,' said Kal,
turning back to the Professor.
'We both collect things.'

14

'I am not a collector,' said the Professor.
'I am a scientist. I am here with my students
to learn about plant and animal life.'

'Just so, Professor,' said Kal with a smile.
'And we have been studying your little group
this afternoon.'

The Professor's jaw dropped.

'Now we will make *our* selection,' Kal went on.

She waved to Thor and Zov.
They held up small cans
that had been clipped to their belts.

Then the air was filled with blue smoke.
'It smells like roses,' thought Maria,
just before she fell to the ground.

*   *   *

16

Maria awoke from a deep sleep.
'What a strange dream,' she thought,
as she opened her eyes to the darkness.

She reached out to push open the flap of the tent.
But her hand touched cold metal.
This was no tent.

Maria felt around with her other hand.
Straw – the floor was covered with straw.
She stood up.
In front of her was a set of metal rods.

Maria was frightened.
'Help me! Somebody help me . . .'

A bright light flashed on.
Maria was blinded for a moment.

And then she saw where she was.
She was in a room full of cages.

In the cages were the strangest creatures
she had ever seen.
Silver birds, alligators with feathers
and things she couldn't name.

18

She looked behind her.
Pablo was on the floor
in a deep sleep.
The floor was covered with straw.
And the floor was the floor of a large cage.
They were caged, just like the other creatures.

Maria screamed.

A door opened and Thor and Zov came in.

'Ah, the woman has woken,' said Zov.

'Yes, but the man is still asleep,' said Thor.
'I wonder if these creatures will breed in captivity?'

'I think it depends on their diet,' replied Zov.
'It seems that humans
are very fond of a food called Muesli.'

'Then we'll have to collect some
before we leave their planet,' said Thor,
walking out of the door.

'Well, it will be an interesting experiment,'
Zov said with a smile,
as he turned out the light.

Maria screamed.
This time, she did not stop.

* * *

20

The next day all the students awoke late.
Some had headaches.
Professor Scott had a bad migraine
and could not leave his bed.

It was midday before they realised
that Maria and Pablo were missing.
Anna thought they had gone for a long walk.

The boys laughed.
Pablo had quite a reputation.

When Maria and Pablo were still missing that evening,
the students realised that something was very wrong.

The Professor called the police
with the radio in his Land Rover.

Ten hours later,
the area was full of police helicopters and jeeps.
Patrol boats from the Coast Guard
searched along the coast.

Nothing was ever found.
The police report blamed sharks.
Maria and Pablo must have gone for a midnight swim
and ended up as shark food.

The University blamed Professor Scott.
That was the last trip he took to Carmen Beach.